ROOM FOR THE ANIMALS?

HOW URBAN GROWTH AFFECTS WILDLIFE

Zachary J. Homrighaus and Kelsey Ellis

CONTENTS

Rigby

A Harcourt Achieve Imprint

www.Rigby.com
1-800-531-5015

CHANGING THE LAND: DEVELOPMENT OR SPRAWL?

As you ride to school, you might pass land that was a cornfield when you were six-years-old, but now it's full of houses, or maybe it's been paved over as part of a large shopping mall. People change the land all the time, making new homes and workplaces for others, but these changes can have dramatic consequences for wildlife.

As our cities grow larger, people come into contact with wild animals more and more often. For example, black bears are wandering into backyard parties, coyotes are attacking pet dogs and cats, and alligators are getting trapped in swimming pools!

Shopping malls are frequent additions to urban growth.

Some cities try to preserve their natural areas, like this lake, by building around them.

In the United States, large cities and the areas around them are growing so fast that there is a brewing argument: Is this urban growth positive or negative? **Advocates** for urban growth call the growth urban development, while **opponents** call the growth urban sprawl.

Both sides argue for what they believe, but what about those creatures who are affected and can't express their opinion? What about the animals? As more buildings are being built on animals' homes, where will *they* go, what will *they* do, and is it right or wrong?

In this book, both sides of the issue will be explored as you try to answer the question: Is there any room for the animals?

URBAN DEVELOPMENT

Cities are constantly growing and changing, and with this growth and change, urban problems like overcrowding and pollution can arise. When new businesses are built in a city, new employees move to that city, and sometimes there are not enough places to live, causing a housing shortage. Because there is more demand for housing than availability, house prices and rent costs rise, so more houses are built.

Along with the rise in population comes the rise in pollution. Many people do not want to live in the city because of this, so they begin looking for places to live outside of the city, but still close enough to drive to work. The city begins to grow and spread into **suburbs**.

Planned communities like the one pictured here are being built outside many cities in the United States.

POPULATION DENSITY MAP OF NORTH AMERICA

On this population density map of North America, each white dot represents more than 7,500 people living in one square mile. The areas that are solid white are home to many, many people.

Advocates of urban development call it progress and believe that because of this progress, everyone will have access to a clean, healthy, affordable living environment. Without this development outside of large cities, the cost of living would be outrageous, and everyone has a right to choose where they want to live. Plus, there are animals like squirrels who have adapted to and thrive in their urban environment.

URBAN SPRAWL

The term urban sprawl is used to describe the unplanned and excessive growth of housing on the outside edges of cities. Opponents of this growth believe that the number of new buildings should match the growth of population and if it doesn't, the growth is considered to be sprawl not development. Unfortunately, the amount of new homes in the last thirty years has doubled, while the population has grown less than 50 percent.

Another problem with urban sprawl is the building of new roads to connect the suburbs to the city. What's wrong with that you may ask? With more roads comes more traffic, and with more traffic comes more air pollution, which is not good for anyone.

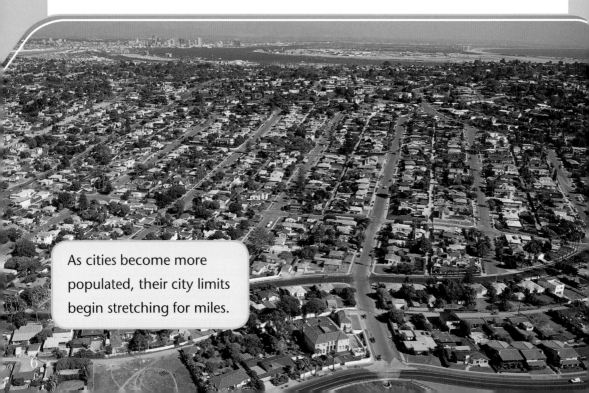

As cities become more populated, their city limits begin stretching for miles.

In 2006 this wild coyote, nicknamed Hal, was found roaming through Central Park in New York City.

In addition to traffic congestion and pollution, this unnecessary spreading out of people over land gives little regard to the land's first **inhabitants**, the animals. As more cities are expanding, more animal **habitats** are shrinking or disappearing. Where are these animals supposed to go?

THE EFFECTS OF CHANGE

Whether you think of urban growth as development or sprawl, there is no way to avoid its effects on wildlife. When people begin building and changing the natural areas around them, they become the animals' neighbors. As with any new neighbor, there are positive and negative effects to their arrival in the neighborhood. Will the new neighbors be friendly and respectful to their surroundings and fellow neighbors? Will they keep the neighborhood clean? Who will they be friends with, and will all the neighbors get along and help one another? Will anyone have to move?

This house is being built in a new neighborhood. Will its human inhabitants be good neighbors to the animals living around them?

This little fox peeks out from its home. Will it adapt to its neighbors?

TWO SIDES TO URBAN GROWTH

URBAN DEVELOPMENT

- shows a city's progress
- lowers housing costs
- people have more choices for where they want to live
- people can get away from pollution and crime in cities

- changes the land
- urban growth
- does not take into consideration the habitats and needs of animals
- new growth takes over old animal habitats

URBAN SPRAWL

- more building growth than population growth
- unplanned and excessive
- causes more traffic and more pollution because people are so spread out they have to drive everywhere

The same is true for humans and animals. When humans move into areas with animal habitats there are consequences; some are positive and some are negative. For some animals, the arrival of their new neighbors is very beneficial and helpful to their survival, because people can provide more food sources. But sadly, other animals can't **adapt**.

CHANGING HABITATS

Many times the destruction or altering of animals' habitats is the reason why animals become endangered or extinct. In many places, farmland is sold to developers who divide the land and build houses, office buildings, or shopping centers. In other places, developers buy land in forests, cut down the trees, and use the wood to build houses or roads.

Cutting down trees and clearing the land to make way for buildings, houses, and roads is called **deforestation**. Many animals that live in forest habitats cannot adjust when the number of trees is reduced. After the trees are cut down other animals may move in and drive the first animals away. Every year the number of natural habitats gets smaller and smaller.

This is an example of a forest habitat after deforestation.

Many animals' homes, like this bear's, are destroyed every year because of deforestation.

HOME SWEET HABITAT

Why is a habitat so important? Because all living things need food, water, and a place to live, and an animal's habitat is a combination of all those things. It provides an animal's basic needs. Most animals can't just pack up and move to another habitat.

For example, a hawk flies over many miles of land in order to find the food it needs. It usually catches small animals, such as mice and rabbits, in open fields. When playgrounds and lawns are built over open fields, the animals that are the hawk's food source leave, and the hawk is without food.

Birds are not the only animals that are affected by the growth of cities. **Mammals**, reptiles, and amphibians also struggle to adapt to their new environment. If we don't carefully plan where our buildings are being built, we can take away the animals' valuable water, food sources, and homes.

Sometimes people try to compromise by removing only part of a habitat or cutting a wide path for a roadway through a habitat. Splitting up a habitat in this way is called **habitat fragmentation**.

You may have seen the result of habitat fragmentation for yourself. Animals have specific places where they find food and water and specific paths to get to those places. When a highway crosses their path, animals like deer continue on the same route and often try to cross the busy roadways. Unfortunately, every year, thousands of deer and other animals are hit by cars and killed as they try to cross roads. These accidents also cause millions of dollars in damage to cars and can cause serious injury to drivers, too.

Deer are not the only animals that struggle because of habitat fragmentation. The gray foxes in North American forests like to live in the deep parts of a forest because they need to be able to hide under bushes and branches to find their **prey**. When people cut large chunks out of a forest, there is no deep part for the gray foxes to live and they quickly die out.

Gray foxes like to live deep in the forest where they can climb trees to get the berries they like to eat. They are the only kind of fox that can climb trees.

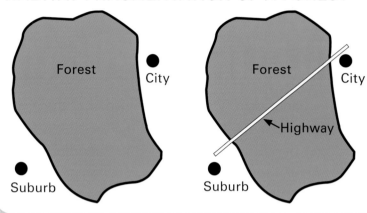

HABITAT FRAGMENTATION OF A FOREST

The diagram on the left shows a forest between a city and a suburb. The diagram on the right shows the same forest after a highway is built connecting the city and the suburb.

Forest · City · Suburb

Forest · City · Highway · Suburb

When the ovenbird's deep forest home is broken up by habitat fragmentation, the ovenbird becomes vulnerable to an unexpected problem: nest **parasites**, which are animals that live in another animal's home or on another animal and does it harm. When the ovenbird leaves the nest to find food, the brown-headed cowbird takes the ovenbird's eggs, drops them to the ground, lays its own eggs in the nest, and flies away. When the ovenbird comes back, it does not realize that the eggs it will hatch and the chicks it will raise are a completely different species of bird!

In an untouched forest, the cowbird would never get near the ovenbird's nest because the cowbird does not like the deep forest. But when fragmentation of a forest opens it up, the ovenbirds, and other species, are open to such attacks.

A cowbird

An ovenbird

13

SHRINKING WILDLIFE POPULATION

More than two hundred years ago, there were five billion passenger pigeons in the United States that nested in forests of acorn trees and beech trees and traveled in huge flocks. As the United States' population grew, many forests were cut down, and the acorn trees and beech trees that were important for the passenger pigeons to survive were destroyed. With nowhere to live, find food, or raise their young, the passenger pigeons began to die out.

The passenger pigeon became an extinct species when the last one died in the Cincinnati Zoo in 1914. Due to the loss of habitat, other species of animals are close to sharing the passenger pigeon's fate. Do we want to lose more animals in the same way?

A passenger pigeon

The national bird of the U.S., the bald eagle, was almost extinct, but thanks to preservation efforts it is considered threatened.

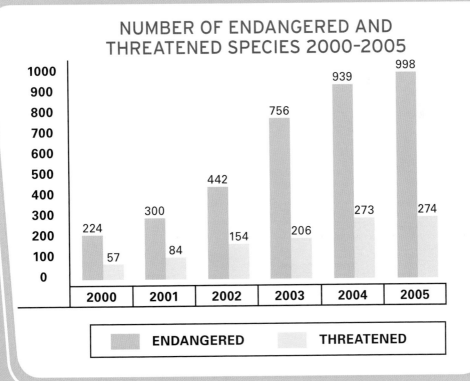

NUMBER OF ENDANGERED AND THREATENED SPECIES 2000-2005

Year	Endangered	Threatened
2000	224	57
2001	300	84
2002	442	154
2003	756	206
2004	939	273
2005	998	274

ENDANGERED   THREATENED

ENDANGERED ANIMALS

The Florida Everglades are large areas of rich wetlands and home to many different animals. Over the years, much of the Everglades' land has been developed. This development destroyed all but 5% of the original habitat of the Florida panther and almost caused its extinction. The panther has been on the endangered species list for more than 35 years, and as of 2006 there were only 60–80 panthers left in the wild.

Florida panthers' habitats have been fragmented by highways built in the Everglades. Many panthers are hit by cars as they try to cross.

A Canada lynx and its offspring

Long ago the Canada lynx roamed the land in New York and other New England areas, but as the cities grew larger and natural areas grew smaller, the lynx moved west to undeveloped areas. Today there are no more of the beautiful large cats on the East Coast. They are called the ghosts of the north because they are extremely shy and secretive. Very rarely do they let themselves be seen by humans and this has caused problems with counting how many still exist. They were listed as an endangered species in 2000.

Toy bears that you find in stores are cute and cuddly, but bears you find in nature are strong and powerful with sharp teeth and claws. With all of this fierce strength, it is hard to believe that any bears are endangered. However, as cities expand there is less and less room for them and some species are becoming endangered.

Bears are omnivores which means they eat plants and meat. This grizzly bear is catching a wild salmon from a stream for its meal.

PAPER, WOOD,
AND PLASTIC
NO FOOD WASTE

This bear is finding its meal in human garbage. How will that affect its diet?

In some places, bears have gotten used to human beings. They have found that humans throw away a lot of things, especially food, in places like dumps and landfills. These places have become a source of food for the bears.

Why is that a problem, you might ask; after all, the bears are just getting food. But because bears get **dependent** on the food in the dump, they are the ones getting hurt. Some scientists think that the bears forget how to find wild food on their own, which makes it hard for survival in the wild. Plus, by coming to dumps, the bears come in contact with people, the people try to defend themselves, and sometimes the bears attack.

Another fierce creature that seems unlikely to be in any danger of becoming extinct is the American crocodile. With their razor sharp teeth, thick hide, quick reflexes, and aggressive behavior, it would seem that nothing could cause these animals any harm. However, they live in wetland habitats, which are some of the quickest disappearing habitats in the world. Because of this habitat disappearance, there are only 500 to 1,200 crocodiles left in Florida.

The location of this golf course is too close to these crocodiles' homes. Now they want to join in the sport!

The Lower Keys marsh rabbit loves to make its home in the natural marshlands of the Florida Keys. The soft, wet, and sandy ground of the Florida Keys is perfect for building the intricate mazes of dens, runs, and nests, which the rabbit loves to build. Its nests are lined with the rabbit's own belly fur!

This tiny little brown and gray rabbit likes to come out at night to hunt for a variety of plants, leaves, and flowers it loves to eat. For exercise the male rabbits usually chase the female rabbits throughout the marshland.

Such an active bunny that creates an elaborate home should have no cares in the world, right? Wrong. Just like the animals we've discussed before, the rabbits' natural habitat of marshlands is rapidly disappearing due to the increased development and tourism in the Florida Keys. As of 2006, there are only an estimated 259 rabbits left, and they, too, are now considered endangered.

A Lower Keys marsh rabbit

Another beautiful animal with big habitat problems is the American pronghorn. This deer-like creature is rarely bigger than a goat, but it is the second fastest animal in the world. In 1824 there were more than 30 million pronghorn in the United States, but due to a shrinking habitat and people hunting them, the pronghorn were almost extinct by 1915. They began increasing their numbers slightly until 1980 when people began to move onto the pronghorn's land, and now there are less than 700,000 in the world.

If the pronghorn is the second fastest animal in the world, what do you think is the fastest?
The cheetah!

"Bat-friendly" gates like this one keep people out of the bats' habitats, but openings between bars allow the bats to come and go as they please.

THE ENDANGERED FLYING MAMMAL

Like so many other animals that we have talked about, the increase in building development in the 1980s has caused a decrease in the Indiana bat population. These tiny creatures were the first U.S. bat species to be considered endangered and are disturbed in many ways by their human neighbors.

The Indiana bats make their homes in caves and frequently have human visitors who unknowingly damage the caves. Fortunately there are some people who are trying to help the bat by putting "bat-friendly" gates over the entrances to the caves. Bats can come and go, but people have to stay out.

Have you ever woken up to the sound of a bird chirping outside your window? In the city, the sounds of birds are common among the sounds of people talking, dogs barking, and traffic; but just because songbirds are easily heard doesn't mean they are not affected by their human neighbors. Some birds, like the red-cockaded woodpecker and whooping crane, have not adapted well to the changes in their environment.

The red-cockaded woodpecker thrives in the pine forests of the southeastern United States. It uses its strong beak to peck the wood where it finds insects for food. Why would this bird be endangered? You guessed it! Deforestation in the pine forests to make room for cities has reduced the size of the birds' habitat and food supply.

A red-cockaded woodpecker

Whooping cranes have suffered a harsher fate due to habitat disappearance. Because they are a **migratory** bird, which means they move back and forth between different locations according to season, they are exposed to human elements more than other birds. They spend their summers in Canada and fly more than 2,700 miles south to spend their winters in Texas. During the 1950s, there were less than 20 of these unique birds left in the world, but thanks to the work of government and conservation groups, there are now more than 300 birds. However, they are still considered endangered.

Two whooping cranes

EFFECTS OF POLLUTION

Fish are probably affected by pollution more than any other animal. Not only are their habitats decreasing, but the pollution in the water from cities finds its way into fish habitats much faster than it does to animal habitats that are on land. Take for example the king salmon. This fish's habitat has become so small and so polluted that there are now less than 10,000 in the United States.

Most adult king salmon are 36 inches in length and weigh 30 pounds, but in a healthy habitat the king salmon can grow up to 58 inches in length and weigh up to 129 pounds.

A Karner blue butterfly

FAILURE TO ADAPT

While habitat destruction is a major cause for endangering animals, it is not the only cause. Some animals' inability to adapt to change can mean disaster for their species. Take for example the Karner blue butterfly. This little insect's only source of food is the nectar from the blue lupine flower, but this flower is facing its own extinction because its native lands are being taken over by development.

You may think that the solution to both the butterfly's and flower's problem is to replant the flower in safer areas, but the butterflies don't accept this change. They only fly close to their birthplace, and when habitats are built somewhere other than their birthplace, they won't fly to it.

The decline in the numbers of the California red-legged frog began before its habitat deterioration. In the late 19th century, the California red-legged frog was a favorite food for Californians with approximately 80,000 frogs **harvested** each year. As the 20th century dawned, the frogs' wetland habitats began to disappear, and the frogs became an endangered species.

The famous author Mark Twain based his short story "The Celebrated Jumping Frog of Calaveras County" on the California red-legged frog.

The Houston toad only grows to be 2–3.5 inches. It is so tiny that one of its predators is the spider!

The extremely endangered Houston toad only lives in one state in the entire United States. Can you guess which state? Texas!

Named for the city of Houston where they once lived, the Houston toads can no longer be found anywhere in the city! Urban growth has destroyed their habitats in Houston. Now this purplish gray amphibian makes its home in rural areas of East Texas. The largest population resides in the Bastrop State Park near Houston, Texas.

WHAT'S THE DIFFERENCE BETWEEN A FROG AND A TOAD?

- Frogs like wet habitats.
- Frogs have smooth, slimy skin.
- Frogs have long legs with webbed feet that are good for swimming.

- Toads like dry habitats.
- Toads have dry skin with warts.
- Toads have short legs that are good for walking.

THREATENED, BUT NOT YET ENDANGERED

Not all of the animals affected by their human neighbors have become endangered yet. Some are classified as threatened, which means that their numbers are decreasing, and if something is not done to help, they will become endangered.

The gray wolf was once a strong presence in the western and southwestern portions of the United States, but it was a target for hunters who wanted to sell the wolves' coats. Fortunately laws were made against hunting wolves, and they are slowly growing in numbers. This is important because the wolf plays a key role in balancing animal populations. Without the wolf to help control the coyote population, there would be too many coyotes. Too many coyotes is a problem because they prey on smaller animals like domestic cats and dogs.

The gray wolf

SAGE-GROUSE HABITAT IN 2000

Legend:
- Historic habitat area
- Current habitat area

As you can see by looking at the map, this beautiful bird's habitat has greatly decreased.

When Lewis and Clark set out across the western United States on their 1804 expedition of the Louisiana Purchase they encountered the sage-grouse. They were the first to write about this small, chicken-like bird that can grow up to two feet tall and weigh seven pounds. It gets its name from its primary food source, the sagebrush, which was plentiful throughout the western United States, but the sage-grouse's tale is similar to the others. As people moved west and cities grew, the land of the sagebush and the sage-grouse shrunk. Now this bird is considered threatened and is a candidate to be on the endangered list soon if nothing is done to help it.

LIVING TOGETHER IN HARMONY

So by now you may be thinking, "Is there anything good that can happen to animals when a city expands?" Yes, there is a positive side, too. Some species of animals have returned from the edge of disappearing forever *because* of the growth of cities.

If you sit for any length of time in any city park in the United States, you'll probably see one or maybe more of these friendly creatures. If you have a bag of peanuts in your lap, you might be swarmed by these animals that have benefited from urban growth: gray squirrels.

Gray squirrels are hard to mistake for any other animal; they have thick gray fur on their backs and sides and white stomachs. The fur around their eyes and on their feet may be brownish but their most distinctive feature is their long bushy tails.

A squirrel's tail is very important. It is used for balance, to keep warm, to stay dry, to communicate, and as a parachute.

Squirrels love to eat seeds and nuts. They can weigh up to 1 1/2 pounds.

Believe it or not, within the last two hundred years the gray squirrel was almost extinct because its land was cleared for farms, and the trees that squirrels needed for food and shelter disappeared. Then the squirrels discovered cities. Overhead wires that run along and across streets make perfect pathways for crossing streets. The need for running across highways on the ground is unnecessary for squirrels, and city streets are lined with trees that make great habitats.

As the squirrels figured out, living around people can be a good thing, especially if those people feed the animals during winter, when **foraging** is difficult. Americans spend millions of dollars each year on bird food—which is frequently eaten by the gray squirrels! This ready source of food can make the difference between life and death for a wild creature during the winter.

Like the gray squirrel, the whitetail deer was nearly extinct. Efforts by the government and worried citizens protected the whitetail by limiting the number that could be hunted, and today, whitetails can be found in many communities where they are safe. In most communities, it is against the law to fire a gun near homes; such a law prevents people and pets from being hurt. It also gives wild animals a "safe zone" within an urban environment. Some animals, such as whitetail deer, spend a lot of time near human houses.

There is another benefit to being close to people; the deer love to eat plants from the gardens people have planted. This is a great food source for the deer!

Texas has the largest whitetail deer population. There are 3 to 4 million estimated deer living in the state.

The smallest Canada geese are called "cackling geese". The largest are called "honkers".

Creatures that have found human's love of golf to be a great source of food are the Canada geese. These big birds are striking; they have brownish bodies and black necks and heads, with a distinctive white patch under their chins, and they love two things: water and grass. Where do you think these birds can find their water and grass most easily—on golf courses, of course! With its well-tended fairways and greens and its water hazards, a golf course seems to be a perfect home for these waterfowl.

Beavers are best known for their wide flat tails, large front teeth and their dam building skills. Since beavers hunt fish and small water animals, they build dams that stop the water from flowing in a river which creates a small lake or pond. The fish and water animals are stopped by the dam, too, and the beaver has its own hunting area.

Beavers have also learned to live with people. Urban growth has not affected the beavers' dam building skills. In fact, the beavers' dams have helped urban and natural areas because beaver dams do not just help beavers survive. Lots of other animals benefit from beaver dams, too; the dams create wetlands for birds, deer, and other mammals to live in. Wetlands are such an important natural habitat that the U.S. government spends millions of dollars each year to create and preserve wetlands. Without the wetlands created by beaver dams, many species would have nowhere to go.

Beavers use their large and strong front teeth to cut down trees.

Beaver dams are also excellent water filters. Water is cleaned as it passes through a beaver dam which helps remove harmful pollutants and other chemicals from water. This makes the water fresher and safer for animals and humans to drink. A human-made dam is not as good at filtering water or creating wetlands as a beaver's, and the best part is that beavers do all that work for free!

Beavers only use their teeth, hands, feet, and tails to build their dams. How long do you think it took a beaver to build this dam?

PEOPLE HELPING OUT

Many people know that urban growth can cause problems for many animals, so these people try to help the animals affected by new habitats. These concerned people work to replace the ones that have been destroyed. In cities, abandoned lots are turned into gardens that welcome butterflies, birds, and rabbits. In the suburbs, communities set aside safe, open areas for other animals. Many people build duck boxes near wetlands to create homes for ducks.

Duck boxes like these give ducks more places to build nests.

Community gardens in cities give birds, squirrels, and butterflies places to call home.

After people rebuild habitats, they introduce an animal to its new home; then scientists and volunteers carefully study the animals to make sure that they have everything they need. After the animals have reproduced and lived in the new habitat for a while, the reintroduction is considered a success. Because of efforts like these many animals like the squirrel, deer, and beaver have been saved from becoming endangered.

Even small creatures, like the Palo Verdes blue butterfly, can benefit from living in urban environments. The Palos Verdes blue butterfly was on the endangered species list, and it was even believed to be extinct for many years. But one day about 15 years ago, a scientist found a tiny **colony** of the butterflies living near a fuel storage area in an urban part of California. The scientists and community rebuilt the butterfly's habitat by planting trees and bushes for the butterfly to live in and then moved the remaining butterflies to their new home. The butterflies thrived in their new urban habitat.

Some animals have adapted so well to the cities that they make their homes there. Take, for example, the Mexican free-tailed bat that lives in areas across North and South America. These bats usually live in caves where they hang upside down to sleep during the day and awake at night to hunt insects.

One colony of Mexican free-tailed bats lives in Austin, Texas. This colony lives under the Congress Street Bridge in the center of the city. When people first noticed the bats, they became scared and wanted the city to poison the bats which would have killed thousands of them.

Every night during the summer many people gather on the Congress Street Bridge in Austin to watch the bats take flight.

Before the city could decide what to do, a bat expert stepped in and explained to the city leaders that the bats were not harmful. Once the city was convinced about what amazing animals the bats were, the bats were allowed to keep their new home.

The 1.5 million bats living in Austin is the largest colony of bats to live in an urban environment. Every night between the months of March and November, the bats help the people of Austin by eating 30,000 pounds of insects! The bats have done more than just stop insects from bothering people. They have also prevented insects from hurting the crops grown around Austin, which saves farmers from having to use chemicals to kill the insects.

The story of the peregrine falcon is another great urban growth success story. These swift birds are one of nature's fastest creatures. They are able to reach speeds of up to 200 mph when they dive through the air.

Starting in the late 1940s, these birds began to suffer from the effects of widespread pesticide use. The falcons did not eat the pesticides directly; instead, the chemicals collected in the bodies of the animals they ate, and therefore, the falcons were affected. The pesticides caused the birds to lay eggs that had very thin shells and when the parents sat on the eggs, they were crushed.

A peregrine falcon

In the 1980s and 1990s, scientists were able to raise peregrine falcons in captivity. They placed them in release boxes on the roofs of tall buildings because the buildings were similar to the high cliffs that the falcons nest on in the wild.

This program has worked well, and people are now breeding peregrine falcons in New York City, Boston, Chicago, Atlanta, Salt Lake City, and Philadelphia, as well as in other cities. City life certainly seems to agree with the peregrine!

This peregrine falcon enjoys its day on top of a building in Los Angeles, California.

YOU BE THE JUDGE

There are both positive and negative effects of urban growth, and each side has its advocates and opponents. Whether you consider the growth to be urban sprawl or urban development, the fact is that cities will keep growing and some animals' habitats will be destroyed, while others' will be built. Now that you've heard both sides of the issue, what do you think? You be the judge.

NEGATIVE EFFECTS OF URBAN GROWTH ON ANIMALS

✗ loss of habitat
   food sources
   water sources
   safe homes

✗ animals can't adapt to change

✗ animals become threatened, endangered, or extinct

POSITIVE EFFECTS OF URBAN GROWTH ON ANIMALS

✓ more food sources for some animals
✓ more safety for some animals
✓ people build habitats to replace lost ones

GLOSSARY

adapt to adjust to change

advocate someone who argues for or is in favor of something

colony a group of the same kind of living things, living and growing together

deforestation the cutting down and removal of all or most of the trees in a forest

dependent to need something

foraging looking for and finding food

habitat the place where a living thing lives and gets its food and water

habitat fragmentation the splitting and dividing of habitats into smaller areas

harvested gathered

inhabitants living things that occupy a particular place

mammals warm-blooded organisms with a backbone, hair on their body, and babies that drink their mother's milk

migratory moving regularly from place to place

opponent a person who is against something

parasite an animal that takes advantage of another animal, either by living in or on it and often taking something from the other animal

prey an animal hunted or caught for food

suburb a town that is made up mostly of houses and is on the outside edge of a bigger city

Central Park is located in the middle of New York City. It is 843 acres and home to thousands of different animals.

INDEX

Ducks swimming in a pond in Central Park, NY.